Winner of the Iowa Poetry Prize

American Spikenard

Sarah Vap

UNIVERSITY OF IOWA PRESS   *Iowa City*

University of Iowa Press, Iowa City 52242

www.uiowapress.org

Printed in the United States of America

Design by Richard Hendel

The University of Iowa Press is a member of Green Press
Initiative and is committed to preserving natural resources.

Printed on acid-free paper

LCCN: 2006934477
ISBN-13: 978-1-58729-535-5
ISBN-10: 1-58729-535-0

07   08   09   10   11   P   5   4   3   2   1

for my beautiful family

The reins were made of words of love, I believe
—André Breton

Contents

Acknowledgments

With deep gratitude for my teachers Norman Dubie, Beckian Fritz Goldberg, Jeannine Savard, and Cynthia Hogue, for their help with these poems. Thank you to Arizona State University's creative writing program and to Karla Elling, for giving me the time and the support needed to write this book. Respect and gratitude to my friends and fellow poets Laura Cruser, Mary Kay Zeeb, and Todd Fredson for their insight and assistance with these poems.

Grateful acknowledgment to the editors and readers of the following journals in which these poems first appeared, sometimes in slightly different form: *Barrow Street*: "Ease"; *Blackbird*: "Breastfeeding across America," "Horses Remember How," "Are you expressing a desire to know me?" "Mark Time," "Night Bath, Sagittarius," "The Cow Can't Fear Something Eternal"; *Colorado Review*: "Cold red tiles. Red-hot bath."; *Diner*: "Please come"; *How2*: "The disappearing movement," "Tweeting the Midnight Line," "Sauna Morning"; *Natural Bridge*: "Originally, the earth was loving-water"; *SHADE*: "Being a Great Believer in Cooling," "Heartbreakingly small when you sleep"; *Stirring*: "Teacup"; *Wascana Review of Contemporary Poetry and Short Fiction*: "I am surprised, that means," "Something of an award"; *You help your cat "face its fear"* (Chapbook, Breeds Like a Rumrunner Press): "The Love Story of Monkey and Bear: Aerial Map," "Pressure-Ridges," "The Silting-Up," "Speech of my lost twin," "You help your cat 'face its fear,'" "For Romell, the boy with the hair between his teeth," "Little girls and horses," "Kunsthistorisches Museum," "Blue-Eyed Horse," "Oh come on now," "Eating Nuts Helps the Memory" (now titled "What position you're in if you're looking at the sole of a heel"), and "Push-off Sideways."

Dolphin
stories I told as a child – they're ridiculous. The frost
on skin underwater, faintest blue.

But above, the heat won't break. In every story
I swim the whole day and they understand me. Even my hair and my knees.
This little girl is everyone's little girl.

And take that idea as far as you want. She's the dolphins' girl. She's easy-
memory's girl walking
through the rough field to water – her sandals

full of stickers. She slides back again, I'm not bragging,
but she's similar to water.
How much is too much – she's stretched out more than ever.

Her nightgown crosswise, not like the night. We agreed

that in Venice all the water should run in smooth,
marble-green canals. And that a beach fire is so obvious. Heavy mermaid

– I have heard you, everlasting-friend.   Your confirmation,
and disavowal. God yes she says to me.

Second Daughter

Couldn't you   verify what I sense: that there's no reason
to be disappointed by any particular

outcome. Describe a beautiful pattern –

amazing. I call it elegance. *Single*. But pattern is feeble
compared to attraction

which makes it or breaks. I'm trying to account

for all the sisters' wildly
different strengths, and hurtling down to the center of the earth. I heard a voice say

Personalize this, Sweetheart.

That could be a battle for me – a doddering, sympathetic figure wishing
both symmetry and chance.

I heard my little sister speaking

with mother and father for hours – their rented house by the water;
seawater, diving puffins. They had

a nice conversation. I shouldn't have minded. It had to do

with what I would have said to them. I'd say there must be choice
at subatomic levels – eventually,

the smallest things in me will make the same choice.

I'm sorry
I'm so far away right now. This is all I can say: there's a chance that I could pass

through something solid.

Stallions eat flowers

Double-people
like the two morning glories from a dripping muzzle.

No past, and reckless! Who never ever thinks of me – doesn't
pass through me again to starlight, but, to the first army in history

that knows exactly where it is in the dark. And for them, night is really light.

TV is light.

Husbands put men on their knees – the naturalists
tell us.

Classic example: but we will not stop. Hands like fenders, putting out the light.
Feet up like the sunrise.

The enthusiastic *does, does*.
You may know it better as:

he steadied children's souls. As lying to oneself.

Right now everything makes me angry.

Maybe I wasn't ready to be known that way – as someone who believes in him.
Believes in the neverending curio

of shouldering something. How annoying. Automatically
the reindeer and the unicorn

are just opinions. What glory is, I could believe it. Could popularize the thing
that just answers questions. It comes down to this:

you have a right to yourself. To the *pulse*

pulse of the lighthouse. To the crowded-out roly-poly,
magnificent and old.

Star Light

Called in for sleep. Casually girls flipping in the air over my head.
One with her cracked ribs falls into the snow. One hugs me like goodnight.

It's too bad you don't know who understood you.

Did anyone in their lifetime – see them bare. Did anyone in their lifetime
swish around them at night. In all the dreams I stood, pretty-pleasing, among

the punishing children. The splendid ducks, their goose.
I was responsible for feeding

and of course I never did feed, wee-wee. They were flying little dreams
and the children aged down like icicles. I tell the story, it doesn't last long,

of the girl seen twice bare in life.

idiocy, above winter. It doesn't hurt

if you don't blank me.
What hurts more

is not to blank you back. This is half:
I want you as

I never saw you before.

brothers, sisters –

little lakes

revolving in the stream
　　　　where piracy comes from.

By morning we'll again be like children

feeding on mama. Mama is queen.
Her make-believe –

purling, like the seagull,
between desperation and near-satisfaction.

A nice, long homesickness – we believe
we all love each other. It must be why

we don't criss-cross her air,
deep like the lake. Or unsecret

our lives. But mother

is on this earth – dimpled mud

at the border of water – lavender ditches.
But when we're overcome. When we're overcome

by everything we think we love – then by morning

we're adults. We're flamingos
like the peonies.

Sauna Morning

Winter's sunny

through the sauna's half-bottle windows. Weren't
you nervous?

Just as the world is. How the worst of them
drink their jam and water

and take off their clothes.

It's clear to everyone. Except you. You're not from here.
Implying, without shame.

That must be because it's so slowly. So little
by little. But I've already told you.

I look at the beautiful men. Today my life is just like that.

What position you're in if you're looking at the sole of a heel.

If you are negative over a long period of time
there's some solace

in anyone's falling, spewing
iced staircases. Famous, famous – as a result

of straddling, given

due, given two things at once. The humming
over the back of the thighs,

it's okay. The good doubles. Torture
or any love left over

could be believed. It's the nightmare we share

about the spirits of hurt-brothers, but that comparison
never made sense.

Acts of self-preservation: closely,
relentlessly hands in pockets like farmers

in winter. Tattooed FUN
across the whole throat

not to provide the proof of memory.

Being a Great Believer in Cooling

There's a direction inside the mind
where I don't care to go too far, or into the heat,

too far, of Arizona in August.
Cobalt blue lightened

it's so bright. And so hot you can't imagine.
Heating is disgusting. But the mind

isn't completely bad – imagination's orderly zeroes for heat
            counting to ten to bear it

as my mother counted to three and at three
could punish. Cobalt blue on the tiles of roofs,

the color of parking lot lights on palm trees

and how the blue is solved by heat. There's something

inexplicably familiar about how
it disappears to the brightness – who am I

with my mixed up feelings, like your 'want'
looking exactly like 'won't,'
            your lonely like lovely. Well,

that was exactly what happened: Blue,
lots and lots of it – and then sunshine.

What I remember of it now.

The herons, they made me dream.
Something like that.

I really don't think we need to turn

on anyone. We don't need to turn on what?

When there's a curve in the tracks I can see
what's pulling. Tiny stations with broken windows,

my homesickness – grass-green cupboards in the dream. Light-blue
warehouse doors, bright-blue metal fence around
a pig corral.

The train is heavier and heavier toward Vienna. Red fur coat. Loosely:
       there's no hope for the breath-taken.

Snow all around the train. And frankly, the crooning aren't harmless, either. Finally,
the still pieces of ice in the river

throw a wrench into my doomsaying. Wishing I could whisper it: give
a little warning. Take-heed, or *confidential*.   Paranoia for pete's

sake, to please me even more. To patch things up for trusting.

Great-grandmother Sarah Kunst,
her coral daisy on a copper choker. List of good things
about her husband – chemist's
powders. The gamble. Childrearing places
in their letters. Images patiently into the hands of a generation,
released and safe. Genius lies in deformation,
which in our hands looks inevitable. Light-blue leather sofas
at the café where electric music's
up to the skies. Where the painting of Saint Sebastian walking
into the lake with a guitar. He's pocked
by acne. His spirit a sort of passport. He's consoling us for everything
or nearly everything.

Little Clouds on Teeth

Terrible, how we stare at the man's
delicate ankles – as we imagine Jesus's feet. You qualify the feet by saying

they don't fit. Sorry because cat's eye is heavy-lidded,
partway open – don't believe everything you read, Chicken. Twins
are examples of clones, and both taste like chicken.

Light-brown river – something aluminum
in the palm-tree, like a pink chicken in the monsoon. Like Sarah Bernhardt
as Hamlet, believing everything she reads. Wind blows the tears

right out of her eyes – the curtain
embroidered with reverential cattails.

Little girls and horses

In the burning grapefruit grove you decide never again to speak
with someone you love. Because they're dragging. Or, as I like to say,
your money where your mouth is loosey-goosey. Flawed and wonderful,
asking repeatedly: So many thousands of offerings? Bullshit
you're not looking at that willow tree, I said – and vice versa. Like some old
horse-mentor, careful to be extra-respectful because he was strange enough
to square away a table. And you'll do it too – selling and breeding
as lovers and judges – and as a teasing bounce –
why to me right now you're so short-lived. Why you're slipping through
the window to the mercies of the world.

Blue-Eyed Horse

Can you imagine how Strawberry picked the trail. How Thunder
followed Strawberry and Tanka followed Thunder. Their discovery of the deer-trail

and sisters, picking themselves up and saying,

for the sake of their integrity,

the dearest things. Grass from underneath a river – draws itself out –
it doesn't have to but it breaks

the visitor-sisters. Breaking, even if
he doesn't need to, the trail or the sides of Thunder's mouth,
making her tender. Foaming white

up the horses' staircase. Fire-red mouth

and red nylon reins. We tricked her out of her pity – so obviously
that men were ashamed. She was in no hurry for anything and we ran
her up the canyon to arrive
more completely with the others. Coos,

pleasure that left me vulnerable. You could see
why we called her fucking gorgeous and (this is important)

how it would be difficult
to love someone who'd tell me not to play around with a thunderbird.
Who trusts me to carve out something

that I'd started a while ago or so
explains fidelity by a horse out the canyon – I try

to arrange the memory. To be nothing
like the grass beneath the river that will not compel us.

Teacup

Title: Increase.
Title: Red, round, dog –

dog and cup on aquamarine saucer

with sugar, dog
delicate, chipped.

Warm, nude –
dog forever.

Red and calm with lips, nails
bit, biting the teacup.

Title: Heroic-Looking Men in Thigh-Boots.

White floes around the debris
of cinnamon trees. This is when

I was small and the lake and I
were very romantic.

Title: Trembling
Horsehair-Braider. The whole
schoolyard gone

to daylilies and timothy. Hot
from the conscious, but all right.

Dog named

Sarah-Raven-Gentlepaw
on your neat shelf.

The dogma can by dying

be dying. The air cooler
around the lake.

Hay-ropes
of horsehair – acts

of devotion: step, counter-turn, and turn.

Turn, counter-turn, and stand.
The teacup, wicked. The dog, soluble.

Title: Dog Box.
Title: Someone Brilliant

Who Is Also an Outsider.
Weathered lobster-boat on blocks. How things
can turn so quickly.

The schoolhouse, itself,
like a boat. Title: Worm

a Little Doggy
Out of Them. Title: They Have

Aquamarine Nets with Hooks
with Jowls.

The disappearing movement

Sorry, and more sorry – the loyalty
we have to experience.

Our inclination for resolving,
minutely: wrappings,

white paper ladle, the cow's horns cut off
to disentangle it.

Your body has never felt exactly
the way it is feeling now: accidental, historical.

And vice versa. That we're so competent,
that's hopeless.
          That we're so absurdly
important. The binocular

gaping. The mosquito making
a 'bun' sound.

Just look:

My parents' fragile little farm, marked on the fence
with blue tattoos. I am mistaken.

Dove-gray, uncomprehending
sexual-afterlife of parents.

An odd neutrality in their favor.

You, yourself, have to exist
and just go on existing. Seed-hustler,
the husks –

our good luck.

Luck would be passed along to someone else.
        What we should do with the kittens.

A platform

for knowing what we don't want:
her nail file left on my chair. Wet towels and the gifts

of clothes she gave me. Women
tend to begin with their bodies. Are cagey

about their autobiographies – not precisely *knowing*. Our restraint, toward
humility. And how we've both been humiliated by him –

encouraging each other to dangerous things
at the swimming pool. The unpretending stories

about him. There are surprises: light,
blue lights around us. Waking to whatever. Frogs' eggs

in the water cupped in leaves. Incense smoke
in the shape of women's hairstyles. All week I saw her body

you love, which you talk about: shower-sacks
warmed in the sun. The pool. No one has ever been more generous –
she came, she stripped,
to verify for me – the most
pathetic things we do, not to be convinced.

Something of an award

The gift of continuity carries
something else along with it. Bargaining –

for a very deep pleasure.

Queen-maker dogma

with a good deal of back-tracking.

Grandmothers whistling on their walks home –
you can die of that.   Does it occur to you

what drew you? What came, and for remorse left.

Lapdogs, side by side. Purring and making love.

Then sprung and startled. Telling everyone

how it happened. Her murderous ambition
to become queen

and so on. Meandering, self-punished women.

I only believed them sometimes.
I was completely charmed.

Take them in and throw them back up.

Fly back – wild flocks

who would refuse such an imprint. These are our new measures:
plainness and oddness, – the more quiet instinct.

But we don't want to hear that. Our pups, you know
how they become like barnacles. And your knees,

bits of boat – the patella's tricky oil.

The performance is where something leaves us:
a deep sleep with something,

a guilty sleep that will drive you, and your weirdest
private metronome.

Things being the way things really are – me,
an unconditional goat. You, who have had it up to here

with the corridor, which is of course a kind of until.

Please come

Everything is ready.

I'm calm enough. We're both very calm. About what,
nothing more is known.

Uncanny presentiments
       at the beginning of May. Long summer holidays.

You must calm down a bit. We have this appearance,
why did we call it double?, that has never left us. People twinning,

and then remaining.

My mother taught it to me, and I'd almost
completely forgotten it. Then you remembered

the English word "elk" by the fire.

Everything's ready, isn't it?

A riddle for my birthday

What's more violent than 'immaculate'? – code:
the esophagus, whispering to itself
back and forth. Bright-red throat and finally,
skyward, the bait of words and food. Perfect clue-addict: something
I found important is gone. Two dreams on Christmas Eve:
I remove the body-length stone. The grave
is filled with icewater, and he sleeps there. Next,
Christmas shopping with Britney Spears. She has *no idea*
what to buy anyone.

I am surprised, that means

– after Vinokurov

technique is not the capacity
to make a dummy

or geniuses. The beeping of the reversing
truck. The prettier chimes

of its door left open.

Just think –

what springs – trying very hard
to get at it.

I once lived with all my heart in the *Eureka!*
of some daredevil-bird.

Accumulating terms and surprises – this has been
going on since – well,

the whole world does it. Extracting,
from the surprise,

terms.
And no one in the world will notice.

Mexican Blanket

Certain ornaments – black and blue tiles on the roof, moss around the entrance
to the swimming pool, gold on the blanket-vendor's teeth – simply mean

we're looking for some communal shout. Some heated stones to rub
on each other because one taken alone isn't complete.

Along her arms the silver bracelets. I didn't watch her
every second she was in the water. I didn't abandon her, either.

A modicum of greed never killed the body, – I'm doing what I need,
all caught-up in the impetus of my admonishing.

Ease

This isn't the ease I have been asking for. To be limber in response to pale
sexual ghosts then going back like those fucking gulls.

There's something weird about them, isn't there?

We're all human lovers
who simultaneously snap pictures of each other. But joy, I think, will need
no explaining.

I'm trying to decipher the hex signs,

the self-hating birds, the men. All they have to do
is think of the place to go there. I always knew that
about ghosts. Their ease

of transportation – arising, dissolving. Not wave-behavior.
Or the eclipse of personality. Or rejoicing, at last,

in one another's splendid life.

I can't pull
anything together, particularly. There is little doubt that my blessedness
is a perfect transparency. Maybe also, whatever comes to me first, stays.

Breastfeeding across America

The ones given most are worst. Electrified,
they won't grow into it

and everything cancels. Happening
at great speeds – a mother and a child and cows

across space communicating. They know what has happened

and yield a point in life. This is the whole
universe;   under the mother's skirt –

everlasting. The baby that was ignored and the other,
the first pornographer.

Desperate unstoppable

across her life. We actually lie about it. We live here,
but we lie about it.

A seer, enduring
the watcher's flowing face: *be grateful, be grateful.*

Ear
                    where the sheet of marble buckles.

She taught herself what is to come –
origami animals

on a boat. Those people working,

nauseated. Nobody

should experience anything they don't need to.
Her feelers

take the pulse of the house: matted fur

in the elbow of a couch,
the tipped branch made into the house.

Her metallic eyelashing, and a certain sound –

        the satellites.
The quiet they make for each other.

Crouching wood, washed-up necks

held straight by something without being
the equestrian statues.

The Emergency Chair

Ghosts of choices, inner immigrants, longshots –

one of you sit there,
and one of you here. The extent to which we're bound,
no one believes it. And if there are to be wrecks

redeeming life's epic – local
life to great life – I'd suffer those haunters.

Ghost-mothers. Common mothers. As of Prussian-blue
snot baby Jesuses. Slapping them

as they shape me. I couldn't wait for the man
to call my name so I wouldn't step forward. If you think
of the chair as threshold of some other element – the stone tight

in the plum, just whimpering
volumes and people not knowing one another.

All doors shut to error, or irony carried over time – what I came for,
one after the other.

For Romell, the boy with the hair between his teeth

Horses
tied to all the doors of the yellow camaro. The jar
and what it can throw out
to irises. Maybe you carry the cart before the horse before you can build
the fire that's not just mourning – one
asked me to look right through him. The skinny gift-horse
in the carp pond – lilypads as big as coffeetables. The dilemma that,
in the end, isn't real enough – my accomplished fingers
hold the lips back to look.

Cold red tiles. Red-hot bath.

Hallucination
when I come: Imposters

moving through the desert, and up to the mouth of the world.

We are bent, early and late, and let ourselves be. And hate to death

the nursing dog
who crawled to us near the river – like hedges, the deer.

–

Beach: unrest. *Rest.* A waiting-room full of housekeepers who are
buying, rebuying

what is smoothed away. Who call out underwater,
and now it happens:

the world has an eye. It watches the people drown.
Its nose

      red with pleasure. Its little dogs crazy.

–

At least five signs. Your tongue curls, then freezes
when you yawn. You say *Please, no.* And then *believe me.*

How many times I won't be there – da da da da da
what ends by making.

– some trotting and tripping frail guests,
others elegant.

All of them move through twilight's shell
with stones

and cedar needles in their manes. They know what I need

to live – to spend entire nights
edging toward my moorings. I know

exactly what is happening to you.

Finally, to want to carry the day
somewhere else. Where things dance on one leg,

where there is a Newfoundland dog
for every drowning child. I have been comparing things –

and don't want to tell anyone.

For example, your birthday party on the scaffolding
where a child burned in the sun, and the pitch-dark garden

filled with cats and snails. And I know why
these things only happen to you. It's because there's no finishing.

Because you can't be sad about the lost one, or too happy
about the new one. Later,

you will try to get away, but you won't.
It's tremendous.

Heartbreakingly small when you sleep

Exactly like epilepsy – arrhythmia

plus wanting alcohol. Snoring,
like dying.

As much as I would like you to, you won't like
a memory that has no possibility, or,

is startled.

I will take the sleep, exactly as you are. So then,
also,

everybody wanted to talk about it, which is
a way of leaving me out. No better than

feeling sorry for, or finally meaning, or
to keep believing in myself as we will never,

never stop talking about it. Or, for that matter,
it's my way of leaving anyone. Trick them,

temporarily, into thinking
my heart broken. Because they're so skinny and drunk.

And bored by my straight-forwardness. And then
the memory temporarily returns –

of two animals chasing each other in the city,
and we have no idea what kind of animals they are –

oh, this isn't fair. For that matter, you're so beautiful.

No one knows the honest end or beginning

– for the received stranger

1.

What did you trust? That the snow would never leave us. Panther, pelvis, panther –
that they would leave.

You think something is wrong – the panther, so chronological.
Pelvises, honest, I give them that. We all teach and correct each other,

we visit.

We are all identical about it.

2.

The message stops, and I can only speak for me. I mean this –
maybe I want to stop.

3.

Everything will be hastened. Just remember
that it won't really work.

4.

Maybe I won't stop – these are only ideas.
I tell you, snow is gigantic. Snow tries and tries – I give it that. Very dishonest,

but purely,
more purely, it stops. And the combining instinct stops –

I knew you could do that.

I can barely lift you

You stay on the porch,
they can barely lift you –

the good guys, who wedge fish
back into winter's lake. Clap their hands over your lap

and the gnat is dead. In summer, two lakes

flow back together. And ponies will be jolted

from their dreams of mothers.
Your mother has left

all her clothes for you to pack. It will take too long,
and you will miss everything.

Big guys surround you. If they ever told
anyone what you lived through –

born in spring. A terrible scarcity. Know-how.

In my dream, I send you the blankets
of whole landscapes.

The Pink House

Ice falls from frozen laundry – what will we do with her?
Grandma's warm butterfly cookies

just before Christmas. Her hall's
patterned floors and until the Eve, sewing quilts from my old dresses.

She says our birthdays are holy

and to not ruin anything. In order to not ruin anything we sleep
in the very middle of our persons   and dream what she tells us to:

of the flame of

a flaming ark. Of her street-actor's way of life.

Placing sage at the car wreck during midwinter's
midnight storm

and the only comfort will be spring comets, autumn tornados,

and summer not guessing what we were yet. Father's old
secretive women.

Push-off Sideways

Pan of crayons and candles, trusting in them
the solidarity. Or in her – she's free
not to care any longer. To put out pumpkins
for the bear. But which lover was it
kissed her in his sleep? Put her in a river
to cool down. There's a reduceless
feeling: that womankind
dropped her memory. That six folded-around interstates
make a city's red chakra and I'm sorry it wasn't me
dropped since she touched the chair of anger that shares a wall
with the ground of bearings. Dyslexia makes her holy ghost
polyglot. In the history of disclosures
we think we're all stretched out next to her,
but there she goes calling *kitty kitty*
at the on-ramp.

The Path of Birds

Is it true that the meteor was a dove of amethyst? – Neruda

Cooing   may be a wish.
I think you'd be surprised what the bird wants – agriculture
and girls. *I know 'cause she walks straight into something.*

Eventually she'll stop asking me

to stand in the crater. She smells
like playing outside in summer without friends.

A butterfly falls, she is changing her dress.

Her favorite color: blue.

Waterbirds dive. The woods around are a weightlessness – puffins like fat
falling to glass.

A Window the Size of a Granny's Forehead

1.

Through which can be seen
a star, blades of grass.

Grocery receipts
between panes. Crying,

but crying out – the woman-hen

who didn't last and the white
flies around her. The grannies

in the sky – does this one have
a home anywhere, or is she

perhaps a found behemoth angel.

2.

Come, come
Granny – the boat

underwater with stained glass.

Granny bombing
so everything will turn

to glass. Summer
and winter gods drown

together. Parachutes of light –

the need
for anyone to last.

3.

But not to act. Granny pulls
single hairs

from the sky. Tells

who has been quiet. Who took
to her knowing

and the melting,
correct. Granny horsing.

4.

Granny, Granny, calm down.
Who thinks

of you smoothing

your clay shawl. Your glass
daughter and a line

of hens in the sky.

How secret and good you are –

Slipped, secretly, to me.
You are valuable, disappearing.

Gigantic in the river, until she calls you
and asks you to walk back out

because you're drunk. Because you can't swim.

I want to give that woman something. And you,
below me,

walk away to the shore. Your telephone's wet
and broken. Considerations

bring your mother, and another

strange, ordered involvement. A funny,
crystalline blue. Mercifully, something pulls you – the reversal

of delicate origin.

Men from the women

I didn't know there were as many lines down in a canyon
as across. The memory of my parents' poverty when I was young – the red
rims of their coffee cups. But they didn't pick anything up from off
the ground. The broom at the cloth door in the morning

to wake me, coughs of generations all night long and summer
fixed to gossip. I wanted at the very least to find less possible, or to thank
everyone for what they did for me. To separate the men from the women
and without counterpart, or better, without
anniversary – to sit and smoke 'til I'm dizzy. You taught me
that if someone compliments your pinkie-ring, you should give it away.
That a dog's voice at night
aims a line of cottonwoods to chase home.

Originally, the earth was loving-water

Of a loving couple, the one whose love
is deeper dies first. Fire-ants stitch the wound.

They bite the two edges of skin – the head holds

and the bodies are plucked off. Another reason
we're forgiven too quickly.

The whole world separating us from the rolling whale. From scattering

foam to the river – visionary fish

showing us water. We don't respect our old. We don't respect
our young. Why should I stop? This isn't democracy,

we cheat the poor, and they want to turn the banana into a vaccine.
They will tell you, *come here, let me in*. But I will really

let you in. Come here, jasper-bottomed river.
Come here, sticky bank.   Young hay by the river – I wonder

what it calls, the river. The earth
is a quake, loving and responsive. The earth is alighting –

no right to forgive us.

Iris enjoys the secret

– after Glück

Sugar, I am calling you, she says in cat.

Scratches the pail for noise. She likes the way
I enter the apartment,

and then leave it. Locked-
in, memorizing the cat-vista – of walkers-by,

the grass, orange chair. She is glad.
To memorize, she believes,

is to restore intimacy. To leave
is to memorize. I'm about to do it, Iris. *You can do that?*

O yes.

Are you expressing a desire to know me?

a. Burton Barr Library, Phoenix

'Jonah-the-Whale' the Navajo
lives in the adjacent park – a boy whose coke's so full
it spills onto his shoes. Point-of-view·

his black cowboy-hat with a macaw feather.

b. Walking behind Adrienne Rich in the Hotel Lobby

Beam of light through blue glass earrings that fall below
her lobes. She doesn't know me.

c. Love Is Feminine

My students divide everything
by two. Technically, I find myself saying,

consolation is male and objection, female. Delicate
ends of fishhooks – I say this
is what the Entire American Psychiatric Association says.

d. Row of Three Glass Elevators

The child in red rides them all as much as possible. Brown sweater
over the library vent because he's cold. On his t-shirt, *Falcon*. On mine,

Warrior. The thing that used to piss me off most: Nobody wants

to play.

e. Play Isn't Disgraceful

She crawls through the stacks because she feels
like lowering

her red hair and crawling.

f. Memorizing the Bus Schedule

Child in the seat next to him asks if he's gay. The child's mother says that's not
a nice question. He asks if he can answer. Then:

    – Do boys like red?
    – Where are you going?
    – Home.
    – To my house?

g. Do you mind if I answer?

That hickey is a kiss. Like a plaid dress with a bow
on a dead woman. Raven

and grizzly-claw marks
on my silver bracelet. Fingertips red
red red.

h. I have a desire to know you.

Long, quiet hair. Established that the feathers were the most beautiful
ever seen over that Frenchtown Pond.

i. When I got over being a child

Technically, I'm specific
all the time: abridging and combining

like asking the child. Like a hand between the closing
elevator doors.

j. Keep it to yourself.

k. If everyone decided to call themselves a girl

that word would stop. Dried-fruit necklace in the rain sticking
to her neck. Her necklace of clear spheres.

Remind me –

l. Are you gay straight or bi?

There's a cop to make you choose. My house
that's only one person's house – do you mind if I know

the kind of question my people ask.

m. My backyard is for flashers. Their hands

like rainbow note-pads. Screen door – lawn sprinkler –
leather tops of the mountains.

n. The back door opens out

to cabbage. The lamb and the lion with votive-fire
hearts. There's your uncomfortable metaphor. Living room –

it's something that closes. Looks out onto anything
having to do with carbonation

easing out of clear glass. Heart. heart. heart.

o. This location's sister

is *another* tire-pressure gauge. Purse arms twisted
over and over. My apartment lives in summertime,

looks out onto birdseed. I say bullshit

I'm not hard to understand. I'm not.

p. Love is famine – I'm comparing my home to an animal.

Smells of black acrylic paint and my lover's legs open like the opened arms
of sunglasses. Children back from the stars – their fingertips
glowing out the

q. clear bags of its windows.

Green, practical car. Buildings, like clear
bottles and a line of airplanes over them.

r. Eavesdropping on Adrienne

She's speaking about heating
her home with sunshine. About not swimming
in Frenchtown Pond

right after rain.

s. The Barbara Jean: 212½ E. Portland Street

Lesson Plan

If old T. S. were here he'd tell us *that's*
a different way of thinking. Doubt first appeared in poetry

with the Victorians. Romantics reaffirm the old values. Old things.
Jingle

and recital preserve the lore in stable forms. That's democracy for you.
The question is how to preserve it even more
and get prettier. Dinner-prayers generally disappear

by the time the children are in high school. In adulthood, they reappear
at holidays. Morning-prayer, paired with morning dreams of swimming

with ancestral appaloosas, walked out on legs
years ago. If someday you meet your lover's children, don't say to them
that sounds very Greek, or *gyno-erotic*. When you say you don't understand me,

or that you buy into the power-structure, or tell me to knock down the golden-
retriever-sized icicles so they don't

kill any children playing beneath them, you make me feel terrible.
Through all your work,

riddling history and weeping for three days – remember that today
I'm unusually severe.

Oh come on now.

Packrats chew the saddles in the basement. Fish-oil boiled, reduced, then
to the leather to mend – your mother's recipe that makes her horse smell.
I've entered therapy to understand recoiling Christmastime.
Pink paper heart left
in the book you lent me – and I wonder does anyone care to remember
that I was *controlled* –

we've much to tell. One hard parent,
one soft and sick. The faithful
analyze the way an old woman, and why now?,

handles the last word in the public mind. The way she yells about treatment
until your father waits in the truck. But that is also where I begin to doubt
we have what it takes to live in this world. Marching down the road

pleading *I don't know*, it reminds me: we're easier.
And how you express disbelief: *Oh come on now*.

But my instinct is to be the same. To pick up the exact same objects
in this house – replica of the town, painting of beargrass,
all the gifts I ever gave them – to put them in a different house and treat them
probably all the same.

Telegraphing:
keep mama naked at last. Keep in mind what grandfather talked
about last. He encountered

winter and ruminated. His cornfields and the two fields of my mother
speak with each other. She loses

the pivot. She takes
the tension up from others – this is what I heard her say. We repeat it like vendors
up and down the beach, selling our beautiful things. Selling

glass families – seven in ascending size.

Chakra

I accidentally said *justice*
instead of *wheel*. You don't say something
that doesn't already exist – the way a full-grown man trusts

the papier-mâché parrots
in his grandfather's backyard. Like your wife lugging a large glass of water
into the sunshine. Like betraying luck

which loves you right now, which hooks a memory
to my tender spot. A devotional act

in repetition; devotion in the sequence. Something for me in the whole

sense of hell. It's true, about standing directly below
Saturn, directly in front of the wave, when the shark lifts its payment.
Payment is made.

You help your cat "face its fear"

Cats and children
and girlfriends are not at our disposal

to show them our love. Or, seduced-and-abandoned
thereafter to their favorite drinking-songs.

The girlfriends will be ex-wives of the feckless, marrying genius.

When they're so vulnerable, hollering you're it
and oxen-free. The cats, akimbo,

are over-sensitive: they're real heart-to-hearts. You have to have both
imaginary cats and real cats

pulling your carriage along. (Stevens.) Sure, there's a little pressure
and a little obligation – but why
leave it to the horses.

The time betweentimes when I'm supposed to be learning something
about kindness. A tractor pulling a python across the sand
to fill with air and rise – there are always
three wild frontiers between two people at a kite festival. 1. First love.
2. Who frees us, broken.

3. Mountains.

Speech of my lost twin

In the first minute of my life we told the truth. In the second – woke,
smoked a cigarette and returned to bed,

thankful for gloomy evenings. Three, I apologized for the milk-stain on my blouse.
Lifted from crib to basement – Tornado, my father
had chosen me. I know I'm not worth saving, I wish

I'd remembered that before. All he did was lift me from the bed. I said
'okay' a million times,

do you remember –

the house inhaled while we talked about trusted circles. Remember
that everyone has to suck something from someone,

someone to hold them like a bottle. Tricked out of direct communication
by the whole conspiring world – day follows day, and in your storm-eye
the alternative to the French elimination dance

is monotony. The sequel, like some unusual comb we'll find on Mars,
drop-dead beautiful. Process is accretion –

from the time we are small and accessibility
is obscene – satin tights the color of streetlights. Midafternoon
capitulations shout Who is this child! She's an utterly different child!
And even this is too fair.

Tiger, my Birthday

Had the dwindles for a year (you with a skier in your arms). Finally,
this kindness – *Tiger,*
my father said. I was wayward – lost my birthday-membrane

and the nickname. Dissatisfactions, between men and me,
I've been told so many things. *Sarah,*
now the star is moving in a 'J' pattern – that's why

it's such a hard winter. Step backwards – somersaulting
horse-of-god. Trickling-down
like horse-betting.

Father says it's Betelgeuse. I think Sirius. Faithful galloping
star, this is how I'll love her:

by forgetting principles. It's the boy from childhood,
we're making out on the ski-hill – fire-signs

in the face-down zodiac. Jaguars north from Mexico, emptying into valleys
in Arizona, Utah, Montana.

And the mountain lions won't wage. They believe, as I do,
in not giving a fig. Simultaneous biggest seducers:

chunky superstar babies asleep in their strollers, and Christmastime.
The flip-flip, I swear to God, of fathers and boyfriends –

until everything is foreshadowed. The pitch of the roof
turns drowsy at nightfall, separating

our tiny cat-and-horse scandals.

If night and winter weren't so matter-of-fact,
you'd all approach me with violet gloves,

a violet balloon outside
on the last day of November. O, balloon

to bust and sacrosanct.

The Love Story of Monkey and Bear: Aerial Map

Going public – making eyes. Monkey flying, palms upward

and open and forward
almost like superman. On them, a mountain

she's moving across. Then, picking the herb

that grows on the tip of the fur of a bear. They're going
to hurt each other and make each other better. Well-wishers, best-friends –

granting us some innocence back that we
were beginning to lose like bejeezus

out of us. Voluntarily, insofar as there's nothing that's not
natural. It's all here on earth.

deficit disorder – originality
about myself no matter what. It happened a little bit later
when I found someone to love. I have
a really sarcastic thing to say about the beginnings
of sincerity – get away
from the original as soon as possible like any
ordinary woman, systematic
with my DNA-cake. The longstanding questions of my life: I called dolls
child as a child – my desire
to lift strangers up. Accompanied
by inarticulation, and details of the genius
that would extend my attention.

Sequence of horses – negatives of actual geldings

foundering near the aqueduct. Clinical, and pastoral.
Sick horses swim out for China

but it's a performance. And it always fails. They're opposed,
the geldings, to cowboys.

Secret gelding speech – something far inside them
beckoning to deer for comfort.

The horses are pristine, with no end. Stallions cake-walk
with other stallions

to choose which. The foamiest horses let
their riders off. Just let everyone be.

Let anyone bring
their lines to the lake and the horses don't swim past.

Instead they disguise, literally disguise
each other because the runners know that comparison

is violent. Then
buckers will watch the geyser become a conceit.

Night Bath, Sagittarius

The last line was about a woman's memory: The dog's clear bark
out the pigskin valve. Swishing in your heart those seven years.

Students, in their reasonable moments,
hurt my feelings. Not like bawling in the hot tub, staring at my parents'
trees. I can't stand being there. The blue light of their movie

on the mountain. Flimsy eaves
and troubles. What actually triggers the crying, what's the cause – their list:
greenery, Mary's garage, 21st Century, string of multi-colored bulbs. They're angry

and wonder if I contribute something. Like inappropriately yelling
"Bienfait!" at who's disgusted with the backyard wedding.

Or "Father Christmas!" to the memory of living room talent shows. Boyfriend
with flame tattoos on his forearms and free cookies from the cat-lady.
Insanity, as a treatable sadness – personally, I would cause as much as possible
while you can.

The Cow Can't Fear Something Eternal

Cowboy song with no words
to the cows – the one inspired
by your dream of tying a steak

to a cow's back. You thought her hunger was beautiful
and efficient, and I admired it.
After all, this notion that cows have it all

just isn't true.
If I spoke to the spirit of the cow, and if it were unusual
and impassable – then I would tell her

what she gave up on so easily. And if the cow said nothing in the end?
I'd call her Pan,
I'd call her Vice-President of My Heart. I'd say

Come on, just one night.

The Silting-Up

Painted-over violet. The other version of the story: Why did I go to the museum
that I knew wouldn't have what I wanted. Ratting comb stuck in my hair all day
and love rising up above the painting. Youngsters
pressed against the wall like periwinkles
but at the very last moment – integrity,
and those who endure thinking about it. Arms raised as if on the point
of a red marble statue
of the Archangel Gabriel. Taking something that sickens itself,
sickens its mother. And wholeheartedly wholeheartedly
pinning it down.

The Iowa Poetry Prize and Edwin Ford Piper Poetry Award Winners

1987
Elton Glaser, *Tropical Depressions*
Michael Pettit, *Cardinal Points*

1988
Bill Knott, *Outremer*
Mary Ruefle, *The Adamant*

1989
Conrad Hilberry, *Sorting the Smoke*
Terese Svoboda, *Laughing Africa*

1990
Philip Dacey, *Night Shift at the
    Crucifix Factory*
Lynda Hull, *Star Ledger*

1991
Greg Pape, *Sunflower Facing the Sun*
Walter Pavlich, *Running near the End
    of the World*

1992
Lola Haskins, *Hunger*
Katherine Soniat, *A Shared Life*

1993
Tom Andrews, *The Hemophiliac's
    Motorcycle*
Michael Heffernan, *Love's Answer*
John Wood, *In Primary Light*

1994
James McKean, *Tree of Heaven*
Bin Ramke, *Massacre of the Innocents*
Ed Roberson, *Voices Cast Out to Talk Us In*

1995
Ralph Burns, *Swamp Candles*
Maureen Seaton, *Furious Cooking*

1996
Pamela Alexander, *Inland*
Gary Gildner, *The Bunker in the
    Parsley Fields*
John Wood, *The Gates of the Elect Kingdom*

1997
Brendan Galvin, *Hotel Malabar*
Leslie Ullman, *Slow Work through Sand*

1998
Kathleen Peirce, *The Oval Hour*
Bin Ramke, *Wake*
Cole Swensen, *Try*

1999
Larissa Szporluk, *Isolato*
Liz Waldner, *A Point Is That Which
    Has No Part*

2000
Mary Leader, *The Penultimate Suitor*

2001
Joanna Goodman, *Trace of One*
Karen Volkman, *Spar*

2002
Lesle Lewis, *Small Boat*
Peter Jay Shippy, *Thieves' Latin*

2003
Michele Glazer, *Aggregate of Disturbances*
Dainis Hazners, *(some of) The Adventures of
    Carlyle, My Imaginary Friend*

2004
Megan Johnson, *The Waiting*
Susan Wheeler, *Ledger*

2005
Emily Rosko, *Raw Goods Inventory*
Joshua Marie Wilkinson, *Lug Your Careless
    Body out of the Careful Dusk*

2006
Elizabeth Hughey, *Sunday Houses the
    Sunday House*
Sarah Vap, *American Spikenard*